COLDPLAY
THE SINGLES & B-SIDES

ISBN-13: 978-1-4234-3155-8
ISBN-10: 1-4234-3155-3

HAL•LEONARD®
CORPORATION
7777 W. BLUEMOUND RD. P.O. BOX 13819 MILWAUKEE, WI 53213

Visit Hal Leonard Online at
www.halleonard.com

Printed in the EU.

ANIMALS

Words & Music by
Guy Berryman, Jon Buckland, Will Champion & Chris Martin

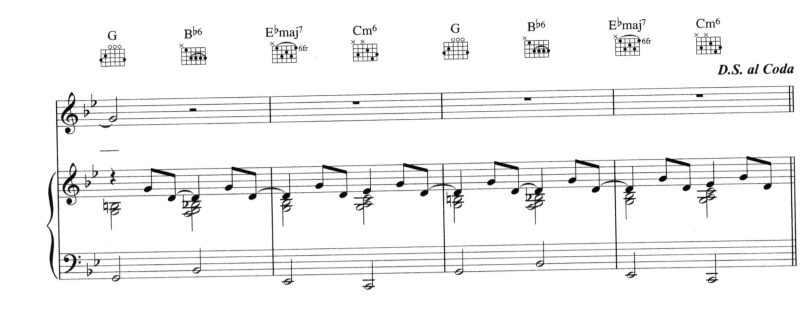

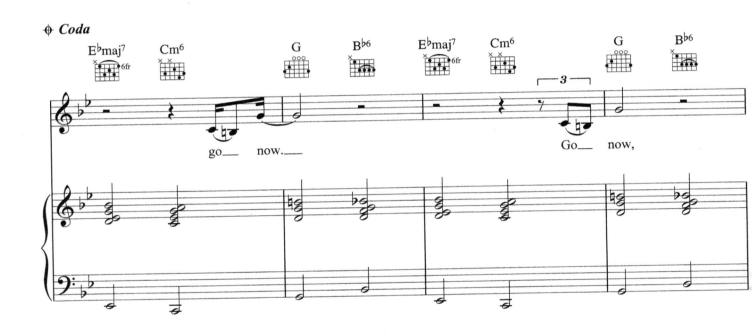

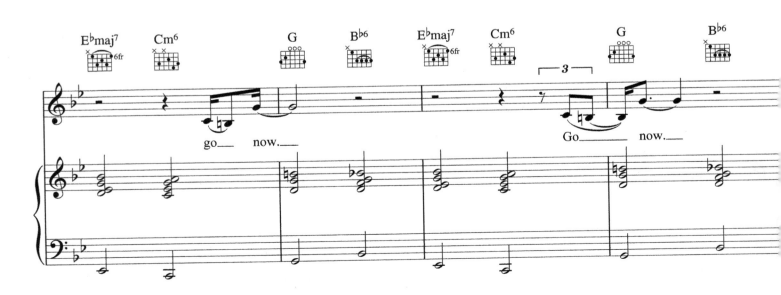

1.36

Words & Music by
Guy Berryman, Chris Martin, Jon Buckland & Will Champion

Climb_____ up the lad - der, look up_____
How_____ soon is now? Yeah, how_____

_____ and you see birds, blind_____ as each oth - er, how long_____ can we suf - fer?_____
_____ long is nev - er? I'm noth - ing but nor - mal, we're some - thing to - geth - er,

_____ We're as blind_____ as each oth - er._____
_____ come on_____ stick to - geth - er._____

BIGGER STRONGER

Words & Music by
Guy Berryman, Jon Buckland, Will Champion & Chris Martin

my at - ti - tude,___ I think I wan - na change___

my ox - y - gen, I think I wan - na change___

my air,___ my am - 'rous_ fear,___ but I don't wan - na

choke.

3. I wan-na be big-

BROTHERS AND SISTERS

Words & Music by
Guy Berryman, Jon Buckland, Will Champion & Chris Martin

But we'll___ be   a - round___ so___ long.___

Guitar

CAREFUL WHERE YOU STAND

Words & Music by
Guy Berryman, Jon Buckland, Will Champion & Chris Martin

and care - - - ful

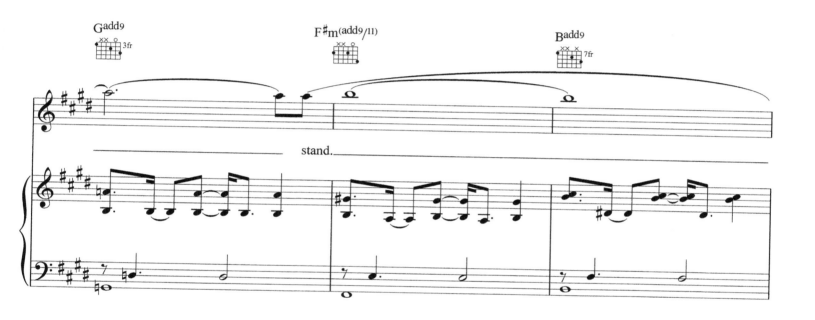

stand.

CLOCKS

Words & Music by
Guy Berryman, Jon Buckland, Will Champion & Chris Martin

And noth - ing else com - pares.

And noth - ing else com - pares.

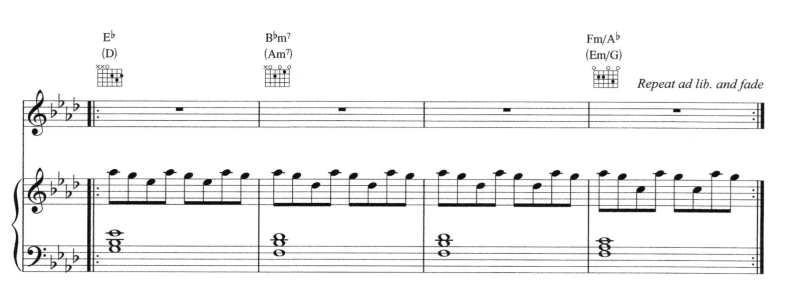

CRESTS OF WAVES

Words & Music by
Guy Berryman, Jon Buckland, Will Champion & Chris Martin

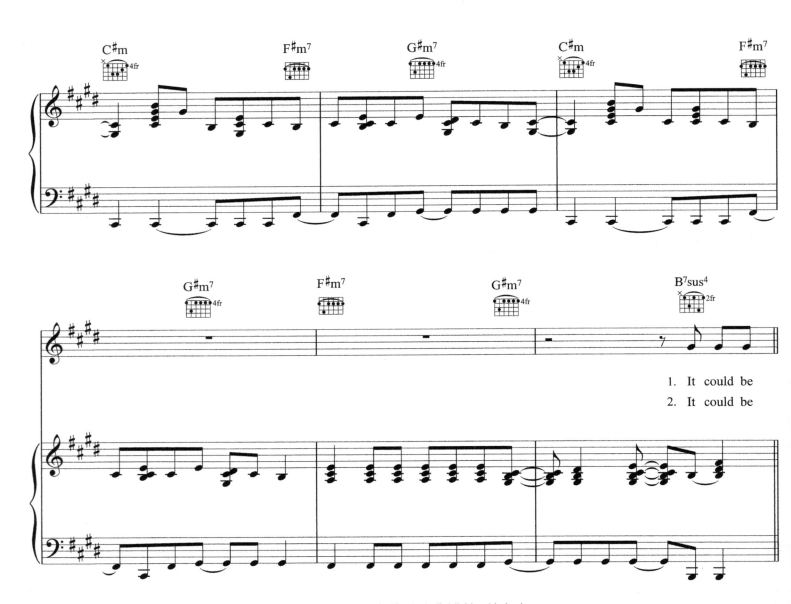

1. It could be

2. It could be

call - ing   out   from be-neath   the   waves.___   Beat - en
you want to   sink   when you know you can   swim.___   You want to

down   by   this   o - cean   rain,___   nev - er   a - gain,___   nev - er   a - gain.
stop   just   be - fore   you   be - gin,___   nev - er   give   in,___   nev - er   give   in.___

Oh,___

and the love you make._____ Noth-ing mat - ters_____

ex - cept life_____ and the love you make._____ Noth-ing mat -

- ters_____ ex - cept life_____ and the love you make._____

DON'T PANIC

Words & Music by
Guy Berryman, Jon Buckland, Will Champion & Chris Martin

EASY TO PLEASE

Words & Music by
Guy Berryman, Jon Buckland, Will Champion & Chris Martin

I'm so eas - y to please. So___

eas - - - - - - y.

GOD PUT A SMILE UPON YOUR FACE

Words & Music by
Guy Berryman, Jon Buckland, Will Champion & Chris Martin

1. Where do we go? No-bod-y knows.___
(Verses 2 & 3 see block lyrics)

your guess_____ is as good____ as_____

To Coda ⊕

mine._____

Guitar

D.S. al Coda

56

Verse 2:
Where do we go to draw the line?
I've got to say I wasted all your time honey, honey.
Where do I go to fall from grace?
God put a smile upon your face, yeah.

Verse 3:
Where do we go? Nobody knows.
Don't ever say you're on your way down, when
God gave you style and gave you grace
And put a smile upon your face.

Now, when you work it out *etc.*

FIX YOU

Words & Music by
Guy Berryman, Jon Buckland, Will Champion & Chris Martin

Tune guitar down a semitone

♩ = 70

1. When you try___ your best but you don't suc - ceed,___ when you get___

___ what you want but not what you need,___ when you feel___ so tired but you can't sleep,

Lights will guide you home and ig - nite your bones

and I will try to fix you.

3. And

Guitar

Tears stream__ down your face_

when you lose some-thing you can-not re - place._

FOR YOU

Words & Music by
Guy Berryman, Jon Buckland, Will Champion & Chris Martin

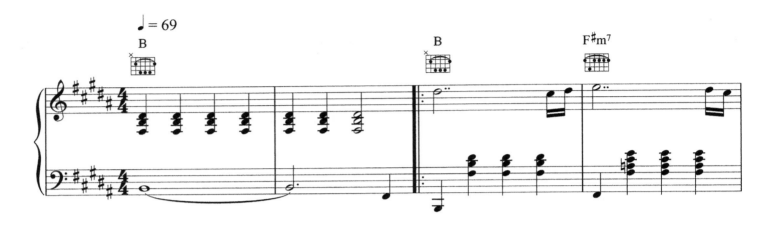

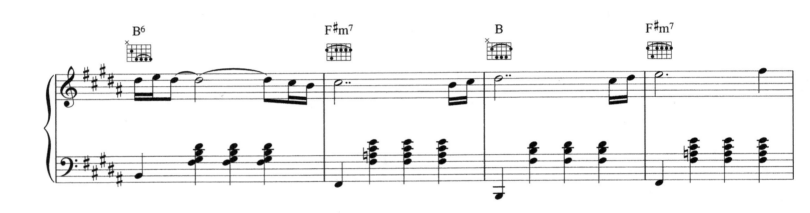

If you're lost and feel a - lone,
Ev -'ry one of us is hurt,
Ev -'ry one of us is scared,

and they seem to lose con-trol_____ with_____ you._____
and your eyes_____ feel like_____ stone._____

Ah._____ Ah._____

Ah._____ Ah._____

GRAVITY

Words & Music by
Guy Berryman, Jon Buckland, Will Champion & Chris Martin

THE HARDEST PART

Words & Music by
Guy Berryman, Jon Buckland, Will Champion & Chris Martin

80

HELP IS ROUND THE CORNER

Words & Music by
Guy Berryman, Jon Buckland, Will Champion & Chris Martin

HIGH SPEED

Words & Music by
Guy Berryman, Jon Buckland, Will Champion & Chris Martin

* Alternate different Gadd9 shapes

1. Can an-y-bo-dy fly____ this thing?____
2. Can an-y-bo-dy stop____ this thing?____

And con - fi - dence in you___ is con - fi - dence in me,

___ is con - fi - dence in___ high___ speed.___

2° only In___ high___ speed.___

instrumental ad lib.

1.

2. Gadd⁹

High___ speed.___

HOW YOU SEE THE WORLD No. 2

Words & Music by
Guy Berryman, Jon Buckland, Will Champion & Chris Martin

Original Key: A♭ minor

I BLOOM BLAUM

Words & Music by
Guy Berryman, Jon Buckland, Will Champion & Chris Martin

I RAN AWAY

Words & Music by
Guy Berryman, Jon Buckland, Will Champion & Chris Martin

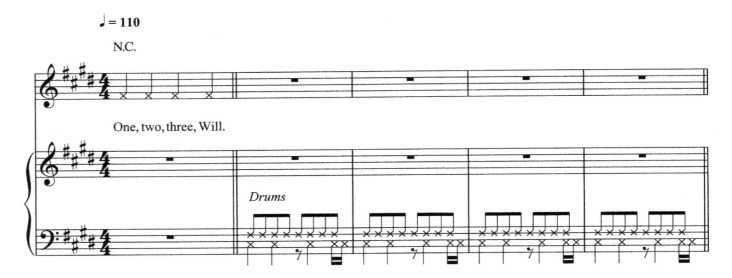

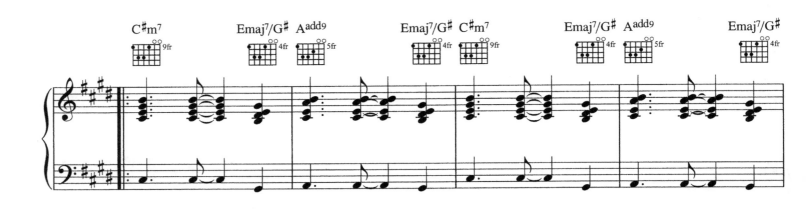

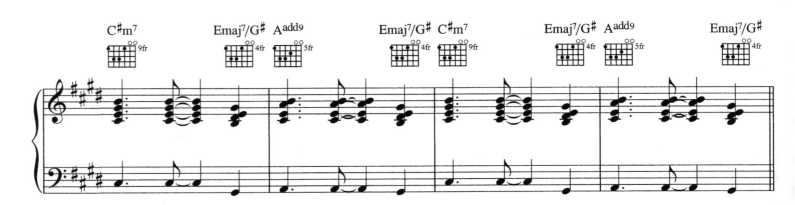

And ev-'ry - one I know__ says I'm a fool to mess__ with__ you.__

And ev-'ry - one I know__ says it's a stu-pid thing__ to__ do.__

I have your love on call__ and yet my day is not__ so__ full.__ And I did

1.

not know what__ to__ do,__ and so I ran a - way__ from you.__

ran a - way___ from___ you.___

IN MY PLACE

Words & Music by
Guy Berryman, Jon Buckland, Will Champion & Chris Martin

1. In my place, in my____ place were lines that I____ could-n't
(Verse 2 see block lyric)

Verse 2:
I was scared, I was scared,
Tired and under-prepared,
But I'll wait for it.
And if you go, if you go
And leave me down here on my own,
Then I'll wait for you, yeah.

Yeah, how long must you wait *etc.*

MURDER

Words & Music by
Guy Berryman, Jon Buckland, Will Champion & Chris Martin

NO MORE KEEPING MY FEET ON THE GROUND

Words & Music by
Guy Berryman, Jon Buckland, Will Champion & Chris Martin

♩ = 100

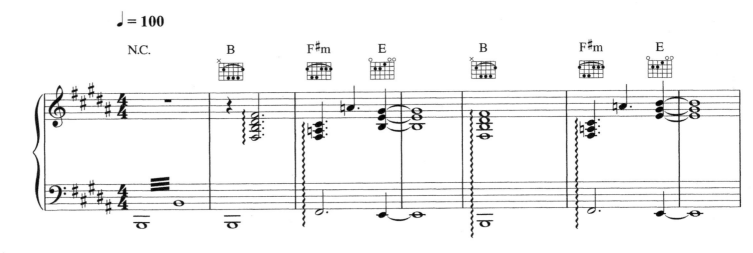

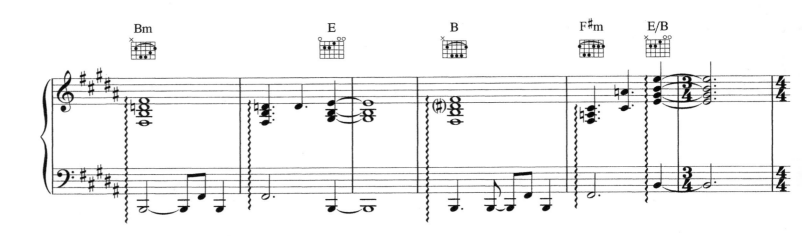

1. Some-times I wake up, and I'm fall-ing a-sleep, I think that
2. Some-times I feel over-charged, it's sur-pris-ing, sur-

may-be the cur-tains are clos-ing on me. But I wake up, yes, I wake
-pris-ing-ly good, to be mov-ing a-round. So I wake up, yes, I wake

up, smil - ing.
up, smil - ing.

try to start mov - ing.

3. Some-times I wake_ up, and I'm fall - ing a - sleep,_ but I've

got to get go - ing, so much that I want - ed to do,___ that I wake_

up smil - ing.

And this could be my__ last chance,__ of

sav-ing my in - no - cence.__ And this could be my__ last chance,

no more keep-ing my feet on the ground.

4. Some-times I feel___ ov-er-charged,___ it's sur-pris-ing, sur-pris-ing-ly good___ to be

mov-ing a-round,__ and I__ know_____ I'll wake up smil - ing.

So (1.) what? I feel
(2.) -right, I feel

fine, I feel o - kay. I've seen the light- er side of life, I'm al -
good, so I'll go._____ 2. Well, it's time to start mov - ing, yeah.

ground.

I'm not gon-na keep___ them, I'm not gon-na keep___ them down.

I'm not gon-na keep___ them, I'm

not gon-na keep___ them down.___

rit.

ONE I LOVE

Words & Music by
Guy Berryman, Jon Buckland, Will Champion & Chris Martin

'Cause you're the one I love.___

'Cause you're the one I love.___

'Cause you're the one I love.___ Ah,___ ah.___

ONLY SUPERSTITION

Words & Music by
Guy Berryman, Jon Buckland, Will Champion & Chris Martin

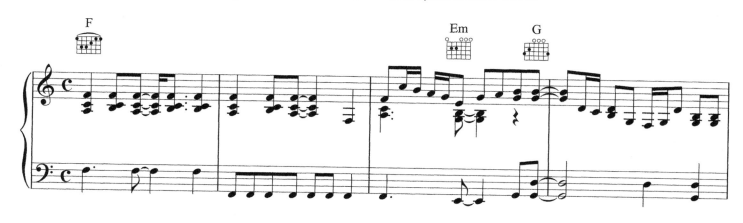

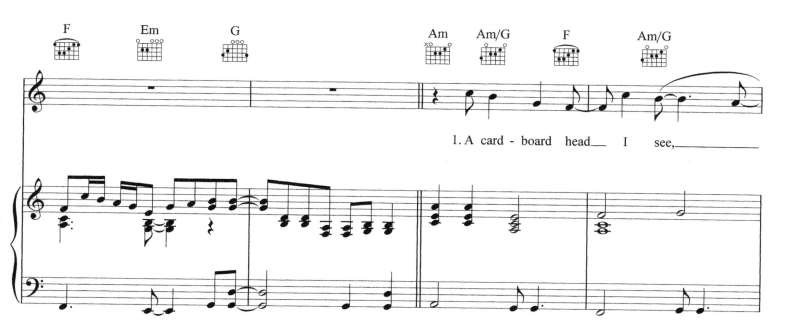

1. A card-board head__ I see,__

135

POUR ME

Words & Music by
Guy Berryman, Jon Buckland, Will Champion & Chris Martin

141

PROOF

Words & Music by
Guy Berryman, Jon Buckland, Will Champion & Chris Martin

THE SCIENTIST

Words & Music by
Guy Berryman, Jon Buckland, Will Champion & Chris Martin

1. Come up to meet you, tell you I'm sorry, you don't know how love-
2. I was just gues-sing at num-bers and fig-ures, pull-ing the puz-

SEE YOU SOON

Words & Music by
Guy Berryman, Jon Buckland, Will Champion & Chris Martin

1. So you lost___ your trust,_____ and you nev-er should have,_____
2. So they___ came for you,_____ they come snap-ping at your

SHIVER

Words & Music by
Guy Berryman, Jon Buckland, Will Champion & Chris Martin

look in your di-rec-tion but you pay me no at-ten-tion do you?
(Verse 2 see block lyric)

And I

know you don't lis-ten to me 'cause you say you see straight through me, don't

you? But on and on

Verse 2:
So you know how much I need you,
But you never even see me do you?
And is this my final chance of getting you?

But on and on, from the moment I wake *etc.*

SUCH A RUSH

Words & Music by
Guy Berryman, Jon Buckland, Will Champion & Chris Martin

SLEEPING SUN

Words & Music by
Guy Berryman, Jon Buckland, Will Champion & Chris Martin

SPEED OF SOUND

Words & Music by
Guy Berryman, Jon Buckland, Will Champion & Chris Martin

1. How long be - fore I get in,_____ be - fore it_____
2. Look up, I look up at night,_____ plan - ets are mov -
3. I - deas that you'll ne - ver find,_____ all the in - ven -

TALK

Words & Music by
Guy Berryman, Chris Martin, Karl Bartos, Jon Buckland,
Will Champion, Emil Schult & Ralf Hütter

You could climb a lad - der up to the sun___
You'll tell an - y - one who'll lis - ten but you feel ig - nored.___

To Coda II ⊕

or write a song no -
And

To Coda I ⊕

-bod - y had sung___ or do___ some - thing that's nev - er been done.___

184

THINGS I DON'T UNDERSTAND

Words & Music by
Guy Berryman, Jon Buckland, Will Champion & Chris Martin

TROUBLE

Words & Music by
Guy Berryman, Jon Buckland, Will Champion & Chris Martin

194

then thought___ of all___ the stu - pid things I'd___ said.

2. Oh no, what's this? A spi - der - web___ and I'm caught in the mid- dle.
3. Oh no, I see, a spi - der - web___ and it's me in the mid- dle.

So I turned to run,_____ then thought of all___ the stu - pid things I'd___
So I twist, and___ turn,_____ but here___ am I in my___ lit - tle___ bub -

They spun a web

WHAT IF

Words & Music by
Guy Berryman, Jon Buckland, Will Champion & Chris Martin

THE WORLD TURNED UPSIDE DOWN

Words & Music by
Guy Berryman, Jon Buckland, Will Champion & Chris Martin

and ev-'ry-thing   un-der the sun.___
and ev-'ry-thing   un-der the sun.___

and ev-'ry-thing   un-der the sun.___
and ev-'ry-thing   un-der the sun.___

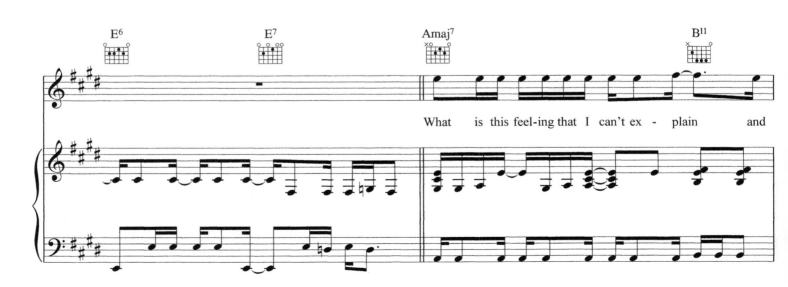

What   is this feel-ing that I can't ex - plain   and

why am I ne-ver gon-na sleep a - gain?_____ What is this thing I've ne-ver seen be fore? A

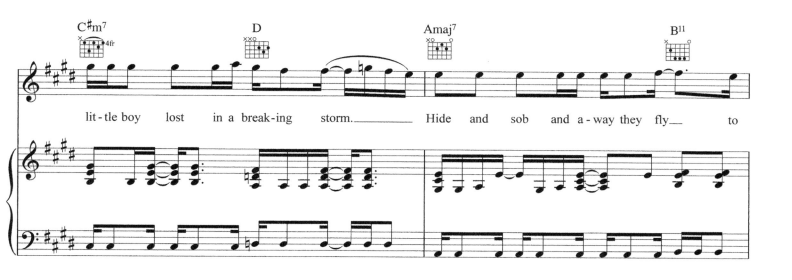

lit-tle boy lost in a break-ing storm._____ Hide and sob and a-way they fly___ to

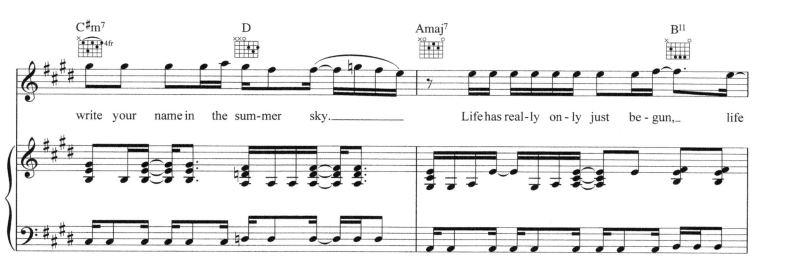

write your name in the sum-mer sky._____ Life has real-ly on-ly just be-gun,___ life

YELLOW

Words & Music by
Guy Berryman, Jon Buckland, Will Champion & Chris Martin

And it was called yel-low.

So then I took my ___

___ turn, oh, what a thing to've ___ done. ___

And it was all ___ yel-low.

Your skin, ___ oh yeah, your skin and bones ___ turn ___ in -

Verse 2:
I swam across, I jumped across for you.
Oh, what a thing to do,
'Cause you were all yellow.

I drew a line, I drew a line for you.
Oh, what a thing to do,
And it was all yellow.

Your skin, oh yeah, your skin and bones
Turn into something beautiful.
And you know, for you I'd bleed myself dry,
For you I'd bleed myself dry.

56789